ENCORES

ISBN 978- 1-423-42238-6

ENCORES
The Colour of Song (Vol. 4)

At a performance by the King's Singers, audiences throughout the world experience a wide range of emotions depicted in the group's vast repertoire – joy, sadness, love, anger, jealousy, laughter. The range of vocal colours used is no less wide, and by the end of the concert the audiences perhaps realize that the human voice is capable of much more than simply speaking or singing. The King's Singers call this total experience "The Colour of Song." This series of songbooks aims to reflect the variety of repertoire and performing technique which is found in each of the musical periods and styles the King's Singers explore in their concert work – from Byrd to the Beatles! We hope these collections will enrich your concert repertoire.

Warm applause resounds round the theatre at the end of a long concert. You've concentrated hard and with any luck you're satisfied with what you've done, and now you can go home. Except that the applause doesn't stop, even after one or two curtain calls. So it's time for the icing on the cake: the ENCORE.

It's tempting to feel the encore does not really matter much in this new, more relaxed post-concert atmosphere, and it's true that a mistake in a funny encore turned quickly into a gag is better than one in a serious number from the main show. But any comedian will tell you that the simplest comedy must be prepared meticulously if it is to be funny. So it is that we, The King's Singers, take encores seriously, and practise every turn both musical and thespian (without wishing to rate our acting skills too highly!). We like to make sure that if an encore is supposed to make people laugh, it does.

The choice of which encore to do is best left until you've gauged the audience's mood, which often involves choosing it during the end-of-concert applause. "If You're Gonna Play in Texas" for instance is by no means suitable for every audience, even if "on paper" before the show you are sure it would be.

Here, then, is a sample of our more amusing encores. We hope you enjoy preparing and performing them as much as we do. Three reminders before you start:
- Work hard on the detail in rehearsals and don't be afraid to change the extra gestures, etc. you might choose to do if they are not working in performance.
- Be flexible about the choice. Trying to do too many funny pieces in one concert can be worse than doing none at all.
- Go out there and enjoy it. The more fun you have singing these pieces the more that should translate into the auditorium and bring smiles to the faces of your audience. Then you really can go home satisfied.

– The King's Singers

Arrangement/Performance Notes

The Barber of Seville Overture *(Rossini/arr. Runswick)*
This arrangement is all about two things: virtuosity and visuals. It is not intended to be performed at a comfortable tempo throughout. Part of the humour comes as a result of the voices trying to perform lines which sound effortless in the hands of an accomplished orchestra player, but are slightly too difficult to sing.

The various instrumental sounds are for you to decide on. It's good if they can match Rossini's original, but funnier if some can be exaggerated, for instance in m. 69, where the Altos can make their answer to the Tenors' beautiful slow phrase just before a bit throaty and somewhat horrible-sounding, as Robin displays perfectly in our current version. It may also be helpful to listen to our original recording contained on the *A Tribute to the Comedian Harmonists* CD.

Above all, this is a fun piece, not a transcription, and as usual, you are free to interpret it in whatever way works best for you. Enjoy!

Chanson D'Amour (The Ra-Da-Da-Da-Da Song) *(Shanklin/arr. Hart)*
This song dates from 1957 and was a hit for Manhattan Transfer in the '70s. Our arrangement plays heavily on the humour of the "ra da da da da." See how many different ways you can do this to get some laughs! The backing parts, as always, must be blended and recessed in the balance slightly so they support the tune without interfering with it.

The Creole Love Call *(Strayhorn/Ellington/arr. Kuhn)*
One of the major influences on the King's Singers repertoire was a German vocal group called the Comedian Harmonists. During the 1920s and '30s, and up until the outbreak of World War II when the group disbanded and fled Hitler's Germany, the Comedian Harmonists entertained audiences with their eclectic repertoire and sense of humour. But most important to us was their ability to imitate instruments. After the Comedian Harmonists came another vocal group, this time in the U.S.A. They became "instrumental specialists," but again using only their voices, and became known to the world as the Mills Brothers. Archive recordings of both these groups are still available and we recommend them to you for listening.

This arrangement of "The Creole Love Call" was specially commisioned for the King's Singers album *A Tribute to the Comedian Harmonists*, which was recorded back in the mid-'80s, and has become a favourite with audiences across the world.

When performing this piece we don't simply imitate instruments, but really believe we're a small "laid back" jazz "combo" – with a sense of humour! Often we perform with our eyes tightly closed, almost playing for ourselves, but inviting the audience into our small, intimate jazz club. We are constantly evolving the way this piece is performed, experimenting with the instruments/sounds we use. What works best for you is the way to go. So don't be tied to the sounds written on the page – they're only a guide. Remember, experiment and have fun!

Honey Pie *(Lennon/McCartney/arr. Hart)*
This is one of the all-time classic and brilliant arrangements that we have in our repertoire and certainly shows Paul Hart, the arranger, at his best. Rumour has it that he used to write some of his best arrangements from the back of a London cab, zipping between recording sessions. It is fun and frolics from the very first stanza to the last. Having said that, it will really pay off if you spend time getting everything right! As well as getting the correct notes, take time to work on the accompaniment to the solos. Make sure that this is perfectly balanced, with all the chords sounding true. Make sure the sounds are the same throughout the parts. Take the music seriously… but not yourselves. You can never give this piece too much energy! Try it! Have fun!!

I Know an Old Lady (There Was an Old Lady Who Swallowed a Fly)
(Bonne/Mills/arr. Runswick)
This is a great fun piece to sing, but choirs must be prepared to give their all to the performance. It will only look funny if the choral parts are very tightly sung, well-together and done with a straight face. This will contrast with the animal sounds (to be made after each animal is announced), which should never be self-conscious and always enthusiastic! We recommend that the tempo increases as the piece goes on, which adds to the dramatic effect. Also, be careful with the timing of the ending, given that by this time everyone in the audience should be laughing so much they could miss the joke!

If You're Gonna Play in Texas (You Gotta Have a Fiddle in the Band)
(Mitchell/Kellum/arr. Hart)
This is a piece where we like to let our hair down (those of us who still have some!). It relies on some well worked out stagecraft – you might consider for example imitating instruments, dancing and putting on an outrageous Texan accent. Be careful though that in all these efforts the sound does not fragment. The top parts must always be able to hear the energised bass. Keep up the vocal energy, look like you are having fun, and this piece will be a real winner. If you are lucky, people in the audience will wave their little and index fingers at you, whilst giving off loud yelps of approval!

Ob-la-di, Ob-la-da *(Lennon/McCartney/arr. Ives)*
This is a fun arrangement for choirs. Make sure that the accompanying parts let the melody through – a common mistake, and worth spending time on in rehearsal. Also, experiment with different sounds to make the introduction funny. We have always just stuck our fingers in our mouths and "waggled" them from side to side, but this may not work for larger groups with multiple voices on each part. Good luck, and enjoy performing this iconic twentieth century song!

The Pirate King *(Gilbert/Sullivan/arr. Chilcott)*
This is one of Bob Chilcott's great arrangements for the group's Gilbert and Sullivan album *Here's a Howdy Do!*, dating back to the early 1990s (which has a marvellous cover photo of the group dressed as famous characters from the operettas, including Stephen as a suitably scary Pirate King). Forget the original G & S version and enjoy the arranger's more modern take on this fine melody by Arthur Sullivan. Bob describes the piece as a Pirate Stomp, so keep the tempo in check and give the accompanying patterns a good deal of weight. Lastly, take care to allow W. S. Gilbert's wonderful text to be heard by your audience.

Seaside Rendezvous *(Mercury/arr. Hart)*
Stephen Connolly, our bass, is a big fan of the English group Queen and suggested for a long time that we do this song. The arrangement is a classic by Paul Hart – witty, inventive and brilliantly voiced. It has a great twenties feel to it and has been a firm favourite with our audiences from the time that we first sang it. We recorded it on our album *Good Vibrations* in 1991. The piece was conceived as a pastiche, so it should not be taken too seriously.

In this arrangement the melody shifts from part to part throughout, so you always need to clearly define between the moments when you have the tune and those where you are accompanying someone else. When part of the accompaniment, don't overbalance the tune, keeping the voicing tight and crisp while paying attention to intonation. When singing the various solo lines, don't feel you have to stick to the printed notes. A little "parlando" characterization works well for these passages, especially if you can use a funny voice and really act them out. Perhaps even imagine yourself wearing a striped blazer and a straw hat and singing through a megaphone. Listening to the original Queen version will be very helpful. Above all, have lots of fun with this!

(P.S. If you've seen our version live or listened to our recording, you might remember the rather vulgar "raspberry" sound at the end of the kazoo section. We'll leave this up to your discretion!)

The Barber of Seville Overture

For SATTBB a cappella

Performance Time: Approx. 3:20

**Arranged by
DARYL RUNSWICK**

**Music by
GIOACCHINO ROSSINI**

* Optional Alto

ENCORES (The Colour of Song – Vol. 4)

Bah bah bah bah bah bah bah   bah-yah bah-yah bah-yah bah-yah
Bah bah bah bah bah bah bah   bah-yah bah-yah bah-yah bah-yah
Bah _____ (etc.)   bah-yah bah-yah bah-yah bah-yah
Bah _____ (etc.)   bah-yah bah-yah bah-yah bah-yah
bm   bah _____ (etc.)   bah-yah bah-yah bah-yah bah-yah
bm   bah _____ (etc.)   bah-yah bah-yah bah-yah bah-yah
bm   Doo doo doo doo _____   (etc.)
bm Dm dm dm   (etc.)
bm Dm dm dm   (etc.)
bm   Doo doo doo doo _____   (etc.)
bm Dm dm dm   (etc.)
bm Dm dm dm   (etc.)

doo - dl - ee doo - dl - ee doo
doo - dl - ee doo - dl - ee
doo - dl - ee doo - dl - ee doo
Dm dm dm dm dm dm
doo - dl - ee doo - dl - ee

ENCORES (The Colour of Song – Vol. 4)

sfp
mf
bah
Dah dah dah
Bah - dah - pah - pah bah - dah - pah - pah bah - dah - pah - pah bah - dah bah - dah
Bah - dah - pah - pah bah - dah - pah - pah bah - dah - pah - pah bah - dah bah - dah
sfp
mf
bah
Dah dah dah
sfp
mf
bah
Did - dl - ee (etc.)
bm Dm dm dm dm dm dm dm
30
32
Did-dl-ee (etc.)
bah
Bah
bah
Bah-dah-pah-pah bah-dah-pah-pah
Bah
bah
Bah-dah-pah-pah bah-dah-pah-pah
Did-dl-ee (etc.)
bm Dm dm dm
sfp
sfp
sfp
Bah
did-dl-ee bah
did-dl-ee bah
Did-dl-ee (etc.)
bm Dm dm dm
32

12
Dm dm dm dm Did-dl-ee (etc.)
bah-dah-pah-pah bah-dah bah-dah Bah bah
bah-dah-pah-pah bah-dah bah-dah Bah bah
dm dm dm dm Did-dl-ee (etc.)
Bah did-dl-ee bah did-dl-ee
dm dm dm dm Did-dl-ee (etc.)
35
bah Bid-l-id-l up pah pah pah
Bah-dah-pah-pah bah-dah-pah-pah pah-pah-pah-pah-pah-pah-pah-pah pm Pah pah pah
Bah-dah-pah-pah bah-dah-pah-pah pah-pah-pah-pah-pah-pah-pah-pah pm
bm Dm dm dm dm dm dm dm dm
bah did-dl-ee (etc.) dm Pah pah pah
bm Dm dm dm dm dm dm dm dm
38

44
pah (etc.)
pm Bah bah bah pm Pah pah pah
(etc.)
pm Bah bah pm
p
Bid-l-id-l-up pah pah pah
(etc.)
pm
p
Bm
41
(etc.)
pm Bah bm - b -
sf
Pah pah pah pm Bah bm - b -
sf
pah (etc.)
pm Bah bm - b -
sf
p
Pah - yah - pah pah pah pah pah - yah - pah pah pah pah pm Bah bm - b -
sf
bm bm bm bm
sf
45

* Brass sound

ENCORES (The Colour of Song – Vol. 4)

ENCORES (The Colour of Song – Vol. 4)

* Horn sound

ENCORES (The Colour of Song – Vol. 4)

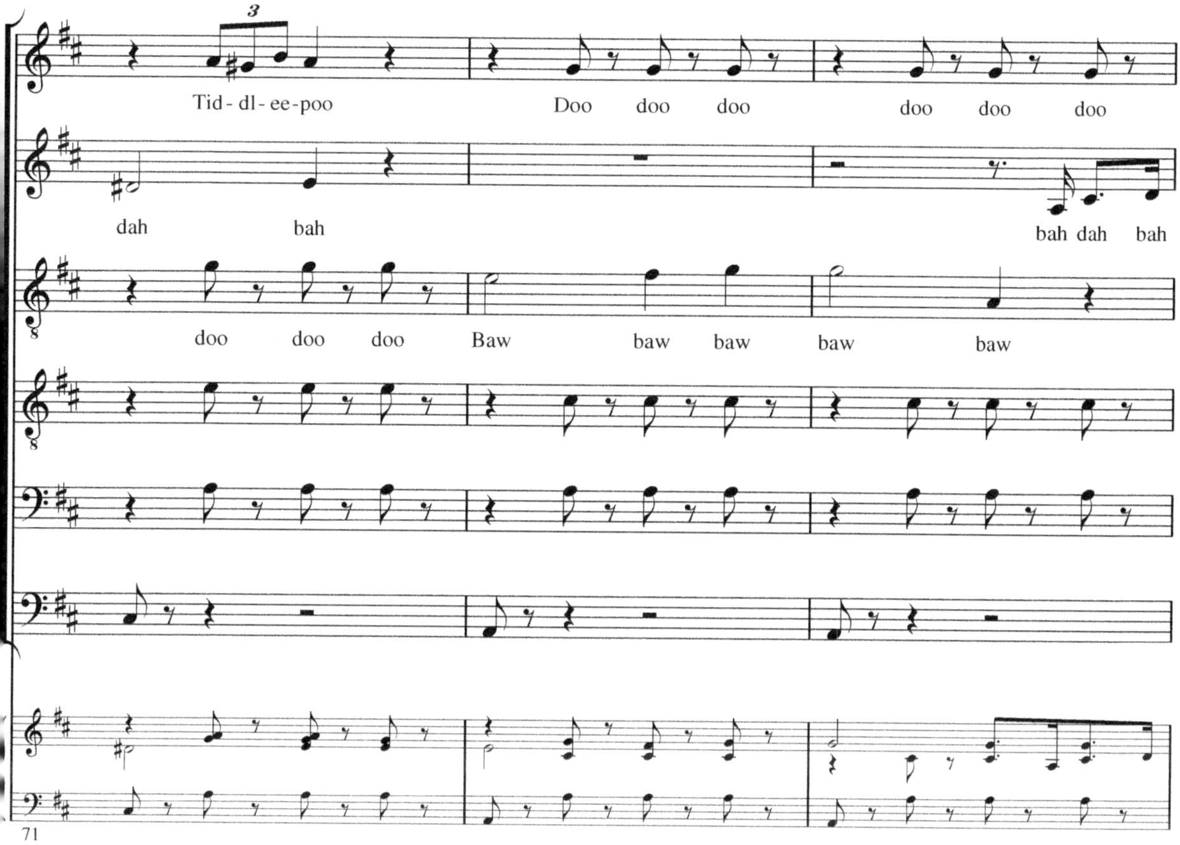
3
Tid - dl - ee-poo
Doo doo doo
doo doo doo
dah bah
bah dah bah
doo doo doo
Baw baw baw
baw baw
71

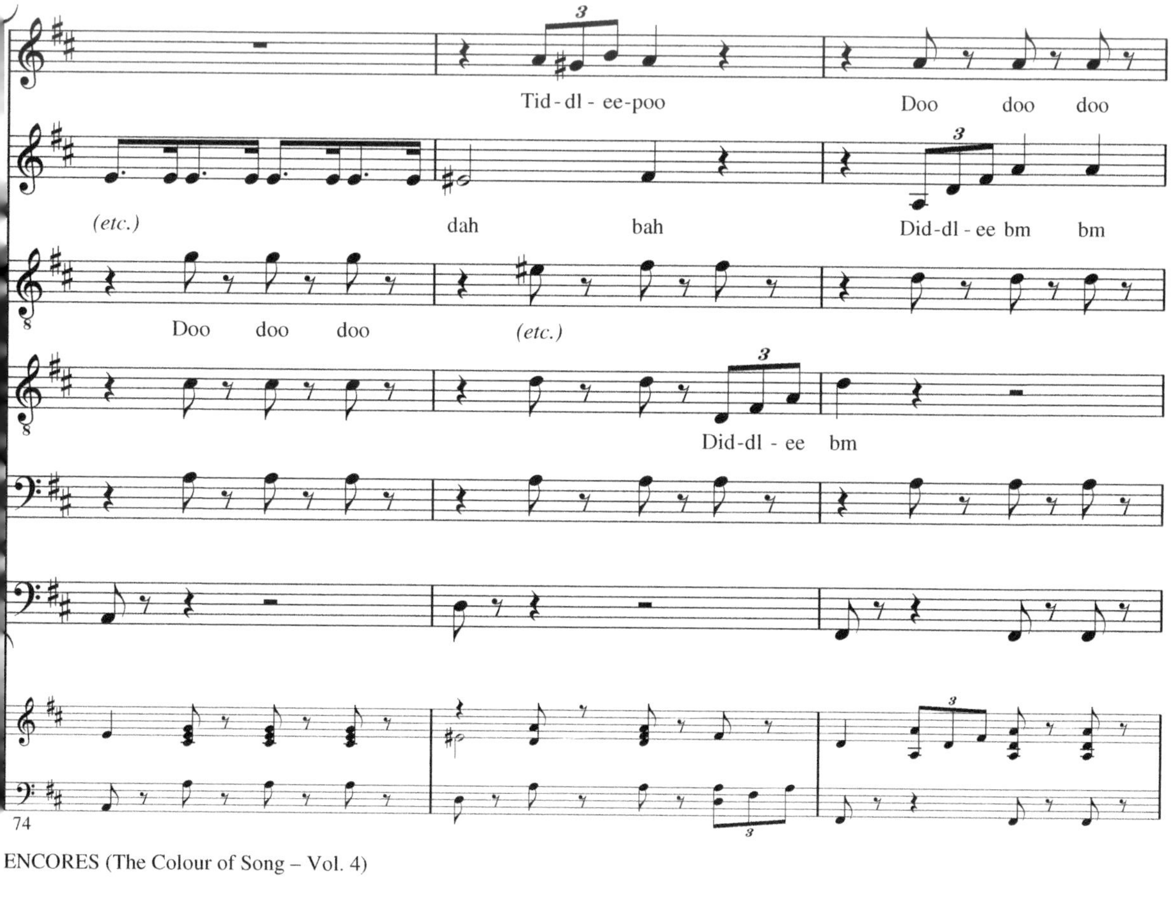
3
Tid - dl - ee-poo
Doo doo doo
(etc.)
dah bah
3
Did-dl - ee bm bm
Doo doo doo
(etc.)
3
Did-dl - ee bm
74

* Brass sound

ENCORES (The Colour of Song – Vol. 4)

(etc.)
Tid -dl - ee-poo
doo doo Brr
doo doo doo Brr
Did-dl -ee
Doo doo doo (etc.)
Doo doo doo
Did-dl - ee (etc.)
Did-dl - ee bm bm bah bm
Doo doo doo (etc.)
bm Doo doo doo doo doo doo

91

91

91

95

* Horn sound

ENCORES (The Colour of Song – Vol. 4)

99 3 times total
cresc. poco a poco
Bah bah bah bah bah bah bud-l-ud-l up bah bah bah bah bah bud-l-ud-l
cresc. poco a poco
Bah bah bah bah bah bah bud-l-ud-l up bah bah bah bah bah bud-l-ud-l
cresc. poco a poco
Bah
cresc. poco a poco
Bah bah bah bah bah bah bud-l-ud-l up bah bah bah bah bah bud-l-ud-l
cresc. poco a poco
bm (etc.)
cresc. poco a poco
bm (etc.)
99 3 times total
cresc. poco a poco
up bah bah bah bah bah-yah up bah bah-dah bah-dah bah-dah bah-dah
up bah bah bah bah bah-yah up bah bah-dah bah-dah bah-dah bah-dah
up bah bah bah bah bah-yah up bah bah-dah bah-dah bah-dah bah-dah
101

103
bah bah-yah up bah bah-dah bah-dah bah bah-yah up bah bah-dah bah-dah
bah bah-yah up bah bah-dah bah-dah bah bah-yah up bah bah-dah bah-dah
Bah (etc.)
bah bah-yah up bah bah-dah bah-dah bah bah-yah up bah bah-dah bah-dah
bm (etc.)
bm (etc.)
103
103

bah bah-yah up bah bah-dah bah-dah bah bah-yah up bah bah-dah bah-dah
bah bah-yah up bah bah-dah bah-dah bah bah-yah up bah bah-dah bah-dah
bah bah-yah up bah bah-dah bah-dah bah bah-yah up bah bah-dah bah-dah
105

ENCORES (The Colour of Song – Vol. 4)

115 Presto (♩ = ca. 138)
sub. p   cresc. molto
Ba - na - ma - na (etc.)
sub. p   cresc. molto
Ba - na - ma - na (etc.)
sub. p   cresc. molto
Ba - na - ma - na (etc.)
sub. p   cresc. molto
Ba - na - ma - na (etc.)
sub. p   cresc. molto
Ba - na - ma - na (etc.)
sub. p   cresc. molto
Ba - na - ma - na (etc.)
115   Presto (♩ = ca. 138)
sub. p   cresc. molto
115
120
ff
Dang (etc.)
ff
Dang (etc.)
ff
Dang (etc.)
ff
Dang (etc.)
ff
Dang (etc.)
ff
Dang (etc.)
120
ff
119

* Shake head side to side, flapping lips.

ENCORES (The Colour of Song – Vol. 4)

Chanson D'Amour
(The Ra-Da-Da-Da-Da Song)

For SATB div. a cappella
Performance Time: Approx. 3:15

Arranged by
PAUL HART

Words and Music by
WAYNE SHANKLIN

* Ms. 7-37 may be sung as a solo, in which case all other altos sing 1st Alto part.

Altos only
(Quasi banjo)
Chan-son d'a - mour,_
tunk - a tunk - a tunk
mour,_
(Quasi banjo)
Chan-son d'a - mour,_
tunk - a tunk - a tunk
ra da da da da dm
tunk tunk-a tunk-a tunk tunk - a tunk - a tunk - a tunk -a tunk -a tunk oo -
play en - core
tunk tunk-a tunk-a tunk tunk - a tunk - a tunk - a tunk -a tunk -a tunk oo -
dm d-dm dm dm dm dm d-dm oo -

15
ah tunk - a tunk tunk - a tunk tunk - a tunk - a tunk tunk tunk - a tunk - a tunk - a
here in my heart
ah tunk - a tunk tunk - a tunk tunk - a tunk - a tunk tunk tunk - a tunk - a tunk - a
ah dm dm dm dm dm d - dm
R.H. L.H.
15
Add Sopranos
tunk ra da da da da, more and more, do do do do do do
more and more,
tunk ra da da da da, more and more, do do do do do do
dm ra da da da da da da more and more,

23
do do do do do,   Chan - son   d'a - mour,   d'a
Chan - son   d'a - mour,
do do do do do,   Chan - son   d'a - mour,   d'a
d - b - d - dm   d'a - mour,
23
Altos only
mour,   ra da da da da,   je   t'a-dore,   tunk-a tunk-a tunk-a
je   t'a-dore,
mour,   ra da da da da,   je   t'a-dore,   tunk-a tunk-a tunk-a
d - b - d - dm   ra da da da da da da   je   t'a-dore,   dm

31
tunk - a tunk - a tunk oo - ah tunk - a tunk tunk - a tunk tunk - a tunk - a tunk
here in my
tunk - a tunk - a tunk oo - ah tunk - a tunk tunk - a tunk tunk - a tunk - a tunk
dm dm oo - ah dm dm dm dm
31
R.H. L.H.
Add Sopranos
tunk tunk - a tunk tunk - a tunk, Chan-son
heart, Chan-son
tunk tunk - a tunk tunk - a tunk, Chan-son
dm d - dm dm da - rrra da da da da,

31
fp
d'a-mour,_ d'a-mour, Chan-son d'a-mour,_
d'a-mour,_ Chan -
fp
d'a-mour, d'a-mour, Chan-son d'a-mour,_
fp
Chan-son_ d'a-mour,_ d'a-mour,_ d'a-mour, Chan-son d'a-mour,_
39
Soprano
mf
d'a - mour,_ ra da da da
Alto I
fp
mf
Alto II
son_ d'a - mour,_ ra da da da
Tenor
mf fp mf
Chan-son_ d'a - mour._ ra da da da
Bass I
Chan - son d'a - mour,_
mf
Bass II
mf
Chan-son d-b-d-dm
39

* At this point any 2nd Altos who have been singing the 1st Alto part should return to the 2nd Alto part.
ENCORES (The Colour of Song – Vol. 4)

da, play en - core, play en-core
da, play en - core, play en-core
da, play en - core, play en-core
d-dm d-dm d-dm d-dm d-dm d-dm d-dm
dm d-dm dm d-dm dm d-dm d - dm dm d-dm d-
R.H. L.H. R.H. L.H.
47
here in my heart, ra da da da
here in my heart, ra da da da
here in my heart, ra da da da
d-dm d-dm d-dm d-dm in my heart,
dm d-dm dm d-dm dm dm d-dm dm- d-dm
47
R.H. L.H.

ENCORES (The Colour of Song – Vol. 4)

je t'a -
Chan-son, Chan-son, Chan-son, Chan-son, Chan-son, Chan-son,
Chan-son, Chan-son, Chan-son, Chan-son, Chan-son, Chan-son,
Chan-son, Chan-son, Chan-son,
Chan-son, ra da da da da, Chan-son, Chan-son,
63
dore, each time I
Chan-son, Chan-son, Chan-son d'a-mour, each time, each time I
Chan-son, Chan-son, Chan-son d'a-mour, each time, each time I
Chan-son, Chan-son, Chan-son d'a-mour, each time I
63

hear
Chan-son,— Chan-son,—
hear
Chan-son,— Chan-son,—
hear
ra da da da da,
Chan-son
d'a-mour,—
each time I hear
Chan-son,— Chan-son,— Chan-son,—
(Quasi banjo)
tunk - a tunk - a tunk-a tunk
Chan-son,— Chan-son,—
(Quasi banjo)
tunk - a tunk - a tunk-a tunk
Chan-son,— Chan-son,—
Chan-son,— Chan-son,—
ev - 'ry time I hear
dm dm dm
Chan-son,— Chan-son,—
71
71

rit.
tunk-a tunk-a tunk-a   tunk-a tunk-a tunk,
rit.
tunk-a tunk-a tunk-a   tunk-a tunk-a tunk,
rit.
ev-'ry time I
d'a-mour,
rit.
Chan-son,   dm dm   dm d-dm,
rit.
76 A little slower
Chan-son,   Chan - son   d'a - mour.
Chan-son,   Chan - son   d'a - mour.
hear   Chan - son   d'a - mour.
d'a - mour.
Chan-son,   Chan - son,   Chan-son   d'a-mour.
76 A little slower

The Creole Love Call

For SATB div. a cappella
Performance Time: Approx. 3:00

Arranged by PAUL KUHN

Words by BILLY STRAYHORN
Music by DUKE ELLINGTON

* Optional SAATBB

ENCORES (The Colour of Song – Vol. 4)

Unis.
(lead)
Unis. mf
1. Wah (nasal)
2. (Nasal waggle)
mf

ENCORES (The Colour of Song – Vol. 4)

*With finger in mouth, moving up and down (Mandolin)
**Possibly with held nose (Muted Trumpet)

ENCORES (The Colour of Song – Vol. 4)

*With finger in mouth, moving up and down (Marimba)

ENCORES (The Colour of Song – Vol. 4)

Honey Pie

For SATB div. a cappella
Performance Time: Approx. 2:40

Arranged by
PAUL HART

Words and Music by **JOHN LENNON**
and **PAUL McCARTNEY**

* The solo marking is optional. If this and subsequent sections marked solo are being sung as such,
  the other Tenors may join the 2nd Altos or 1st Basses during these sections.

10
ww - ahh
dm dm dm doo doo doo __ dm ww - ahh
home. Oh, Hon-ey Pie, __ my po - si - tion is
dm dm (etc.)
doo doo doo __ dm dm dm (etc.)
10
14
ww - ahh ww - ahh
dm ww - ahh dm dm ww - ahh
trag - ic, __ come and show __ me the mag - ic __ of your Hol-ly-wood
14

ENCORES (The Colour of Song – Vol. 4)

26
knee. Tee tee tee, doo oo - wah
knee. Tee tee tee, doo oo - wah
(Tutti) (Solo)
knee. Tee tee tee, Oh, Hon-ey Pie, you are driv - ing me
knee. Tee tee tee, doo doo (etc.)
dm dm dm dm Oh, dm dm (etc.)
26
30
doo oo - wah doo oo - wah
doo oo - wah doo oo - wah
fran - tic. Sail a-cross the At - lan - tic, to be where you be -
30

wa wa wa wa oo to be where you be -
wa wa wa wa oo to be where you be -
long. Sail a-cross the At - lan - tic, to be where you be -
wa doo doo doo
wa wa wa wa dm dm dm dm fo di ro di doo
long. Oh, Hon-ey Pie, you're gon-na,
Hon-ey Pie, you're gon-na,
long. Hon-ey Pie. Oh, Hmm
long. Hon-ey Pie. Oh, Hmm Hon-ey Pie, you're
Come back to me, Hon-ey Pie. Oh, Hmm

make me cra - zy. Hmm
make me cra - zy. Hmm
gon - na make me cra - zy. Hmm
make me cra - zy. b - d - l - doo doo (etc.)
2nds only
3
mp
mf
mp
1
hmm doo doo doo doo bee dee
hmm doo doo doo doo bee dee doo doo -
Tsh
1. >
hmm doo doo doo doo bee dee doo doo -
1sts only
mp
doo bee dee doo
doo doo doo doo
2

*If the solo from here to ms. 59 is too high for the Tenor soloist, an Alto soloist may be used.
Alternatively, the Tenors and 2nd Altos could switch lines.

* If the Tenors and 2nd Altos switched lines at ms. 50, they should change back here.
  If an Alto soloist was used, they should here re-join the chorus Altos.

66

cra - zy,   I'm in love, but I'm la - zy,
trag - ic,   come and show me the mag - ic

cra - zy,   I'm in love, but I'm la - zy,
trag - ic,   come and show me the mag - ic

cra - zy,   I'm in love, but I'm la - zy,
trag - ic,   come and show me the mag - ic

66

1

come _ home,   come home. Oh,
- ly - wood

so won't you please come _ home,   come home. Oh,
of   your Hol - ly - wood

so won't you please come _ home,   come home. Oh,
of   your Hol - ly - wood

come _ home,   come home. Oh,
- ly - wood

doo bee doo bee doo   come home.

1

* May be sung by all the 2nd Basses - in which case, for ms. 76-77 the 2nd Basses should sing the HIGHER notes, and the 1st Basses the LOWER notes.

ENCORES (The Colour of Song – Vol. 4)

80
da ba da ba da da - oo - ah ___ oo ah oo ah oo ah ___
(vib.)
da ba da ba da da - oo - ah ___ oo ah oo ah oo ah ___
(vib.)
(Solo) f
da ba da ba da Oh, Hon-ey Pie, ___ you're real - ly gon-na drive me
da ba da ba da da - oo - ah ___ doo doo doo doo ___ da
1.
(Solo)
2.
knee. dm dm dm dm dm (etc.)
80
84
(vib.)
fp
oo ah oo ah oo ah ___ ba - oo - aa - ba da ba
(vib.)
fp
oo ah oo ah oo ah ___ ba - oo - aa - ba da ba
3 3
fran - tic. ___ Sail a - cross the At - lan - tic, ___ to be where you be - long. ___
doo doo doo doo ___ da ba - oo - aa - ba da ba
fp
ba
84
3 3

* Same soloist as for ms. 72-78. If soloist not used there, this note to be sung by 2nd Basses.

ENCORES (The Colour of Song – Vol. 4)

I Know an Old Lady
(There Was an Old Lady Who Swallowed a Fly)

For SATTBB a cappella

Performance Time: Approx. 2:40

**Arranged by
DARYL RUNSWICK**

**Words and Music by
ROSE BONNE and ALAN MILLS**

ENCORES (The Colour of Song – Vol. 4)

poco allarg.
ten.
7
a tempo
swal-lowed a fly.
I
know an old la - dy who
swal-lowed a fly.
I
know a la - dy
swal-lowed a fly.
I
know a la - dy
swal-lowed a fly.
I
know a la - dy
swal-lowed a fly.
I
know a la - dy
Per - haps she'll die.
I
know a la - dy
poco allarg.
poco allarg.
poco allarg.
poco allarg.
poco allarg.
ten.
ten.
ten.
ten.
ten.
a tempo
a tempo
a tempo
a tempo
a tempo
11
poco allarg.
a tempo
swal-lowed
Oo
Ah
She swal-lowed the spi-der to
swal-lowed
Oo
Ah
She swal-lowed spi-der
swal-lowed
Oo
Ah
She swal-lowed spi-der
swal-lowed
Oo
Ah
She swal-lowed spi-der
swal-lowed a spi-der that
wrig-gled and jig-gled and
tick-led in-side her. She
swal-lowed spi-der
swal-lowed
Oo
Ah
She swal-lowed spi-der
poco allarg.
poco allarg.
poco allarg.
poco allarg.
poco allarg.
a tempo
a tempo
a tempo
a tempo
a tempo

catch the fly. I don't know why she swal-lowed a fly.
catch fly. I don't know why she swal-lowed a fly.
catch fly. I don't know why she swal-lowed a fly.
catch fly. I don't know why she swal-lowed a fly.
catch fly. I don't know why she swal-lowed a fly.
catch fly. I don't know why Per - haps she'll
I know an old la - dy who swal-lowed Ah
I know a la - dy swal-lowed Ah
I know a la - dy swal-lowed Ah
I know a la - dy swal-lowed a bird. Oh how ab-surd to
I know a la - dy swal-lowed Ah
die. I know a la - dy swal-lowed Ah
poco allarg.
ten. a tempo poco allarg.

21
a tempo
poco allarg.
Ah swa - bir - ca - spi - Oo
a tempo
poco allarg.
Ah swa - bir - ca - spi - Oo
a tempo
poco allarg.
Ah swa - bir - ca - spi - Oo
a tempo
poco allarg.
swal-low a bird. She swal-lowed the bird to catch the Oo
a tempo
poco allarg.
Ah swa - bir - ca - spi-der that wrig-gled and jig-gled and
a tempo
poco allarg.
Ah swa - bir - ca - spi - Oo
21
a tempo
poco allarg.
20
25
a tempo
Ah She swal-lowed the spi-der to catch the fly. I don't know why she
a tempo
Ah She swal-lowed spi-der catch fly. I don't know why she
a tempo
Ah She swal-lowed spi-der catch fly. I don't know why she
a tempo
Ah She swal-lowed spi-der catch fly. I don't know why she
a tempo
tick-led in-side her. She swal-lowed spi-der catch fly. I don't know why she
a tempo
Ah She swal-lowed spi-der catch fly. I don't know why
25
a tempo
24

poco allarg.
ten.
31
a tempo
swal-lowed a fly.
I
know an old la-dy who
poco allarg.
ten.
a tempo
swal-lowed a fly.
I
know a la-dy
poco allarg.
ten.
a tempo
swal-lowed a fly.
I
know a la-dy
poco allarg.
ten.
a tempo
swal-lowed a fly.
I
know a la-dy
poco allarg.
ten.
a tempo
swal-lowed a fly.
I
know a la-dy
2
2
poco allarg.
ten.
a tempo
Per-haps she'll die.
I
know a la-dy
ten.
31
a tempo
poco allarg.
ten.
a tempo
28
35
poco allarg.
a tempo
swal-lowed
Ah
Ah
swa - ca -
poco allarg.
a tempo
swal-lowed
Ah
Ah
swa - ca -
poco allarg.
a tempo
swal-lowed a cat.
Just fan-cy that to swal-low a cat. She swal-lowed the cat to
poco allarg.
a tempo
swal-lowed
Ah
Ah
swa - ca -
poco allarg.
a tempo
swal-lowed
Ah
Ah
swa - ca -
poco allarg.
a tempo
swal-lowed
Ah
Ah
swa - ca -
35
poco allarg.
a tempo
32

poco allarg.
ca - bir - swa - bir - ca - spi - Oo
poco allarg.
ca - bir - swa - bir - ca - spi - Oo
poco allarg.
catch the swa - bir - ca - spi - Oo
poco allarg.
ca - bird. She swal-lowed the bird to catch the Oo
poco allarg.
ca - bir - swa - bir - ca - spi-der that wrig-gled and jig-gled and
poco allarg.
ca - bir - swa - bir - ca - spi - Oo
poco allarg.
41
a tempo
Ah She swal-lowed the spi-der to catch the fly. I don't know why she
a tempo
Ah She swal-lowed spi-der catch fly. I don't know why she
a tempo
Ah She swal-lowed spi-der catch fly. I don't know why she
a tempo
Ah She swal-lowed spi-der catch fly. I don't know why she
a tempo
tick-led in-side her. She swal-lowed spi-der catch fly. I don't know why she
a tempo
Ah She swal-lowed spi-der catch fly. I don't know why
41
a tempo

47
poco allarg.
ten.
a tempo
swal-lowed a fly.
I know an old la - dy who swal-lowed
poco allarg.
ten.
a tempo
swal-lowed a fly.
I know a la - dy swal-lowed a dog!
poco allarg.
ten.
a tempo
swal-lowed a fly.
I know a la - dy swal-lowed
poco allarg.
ten.
a tempo
swal-lowed a fly.
I know a la - dy swal-lowed
poco allarg.
ten.
a tempo
swal-lowed a fly.
I know a la - dy swal-lowed
poco allarg.
2
2
ten.
a tempo
Per-haps she'll die.
I know a la - dy swal-lowed
47
ten.
a tempo
poco allarg.
ten.
a tempo
44
51
poco allarg.
accel. back to tempo
Ah
Ah
swa - do - ca - ca - swa - ca -
poco allarg.
accel. back to tempo
Oh what a hog to swal-low a dog! She swal-lowed the dog to catch the swa - ca -
poco allarg.
accel. back to tempo
Ah
Ah
swa - do - ca - cat. She swal-lowed the cat to
poco allarg.
accel. back to tempo
Ah
Ah
swa - do - ca - ca - swa - ca -
poco allarg.
accel. back to tempo
Ah
Ah
swa - do - ca - ca - swa - ca -
poco allarg.
accel. back to tempo
Ah
Ah
swa - do - ca - ca - swa - ca -
51
poco allarg.
accel. back to tempo
49

poco allarg.
ca - bir - swa - bir - ca - spi - Oo
poco allarg.
ca - bir - swa - bir - ca - spi - Oo
poco allarg.
catch the swa - bir - ca - spi - Oo
poco allarg.
ca - bird. She swal-lowed the bird to catch the Oo
poco allarg.
ca - bir - swa - bir - ca - spi-der that wrig-gled and jig-gled and
poco allarg.
ca - bir - swa - bir - ca - spi - Oo
poco allarg.
59
a tempo
Ah She swal-lowed the spi-der to catch the fly. I don't know why she
a tempo
Ah She swal-lowed spi-der catch fly. I don't know why she
a tempo
Ah She swal-lowed spi-der catch fly. I don't know why she
a tempo
Ah She swal-lowed spi-der catch fly. I don't know why she
a tempo
tick-led in-side her. She swal-lowed spi-der catch fly. I don't know why she
a tempo
Ah She swal-lowed spi-der catch fly. I don't know why
59
a tempo

poco allarg.
ten.
65
a tempo
swal-lowed a fly. I know an old la - dy who swal-lowed a cow!
poco allarg.
ten.
a tempo
swal-lowed a fly. I know a la - dy swal-lowed
poco allarg.
ten.
a tempo
swal-lowed a fly. I know a la - dy swal-lowed
poco allarg.
ten.
a tempo
swal-lowed a fly. I know an old la - dy who swal-lowed
poco allarg.
ten.
a tempo
swal-lowed a fly. I know a la - dy swal-lowed
poco allarg.
ten.
a tempo
Per-haps she'll die. I know a la - dy swal-lowed
ten.
65
a tempo
poco allarg.
ten.
a tempo
62
69
allarg.
accel. back to tempo
I don't know how she swal-lowed a cow! She swal-lowed the cow to catch the
allarg.
accel. back to tempo
I don't know how she swal-lowed a cow! swa - cow - ca - dog. She
allarg.
accel. back to tempo
I don't know how she swal-lowed a cow! swa - cow - ca - do -
allarg.
accel. back to tempo
I don't know how she swal-lowed a cow! swa - cow - ca - do -
allarg.
accel. back to tempo
I don't know how she swal-lowed a cow! swa - cow - ca - do -
allarg.
accel. back to tempo
I don't know how she swal-lowed a cow! swa - cow - ca - do -
69
allarg.
accel. back to tempo
67

swa - do ca - ca - swa - ca - ca - bir - swa - bir -
swal-lowed the dog to catch the swa - ca - ca - bir - swa - bir -
swa - do ca - cat. She swal-lowed the cat to catch the swa - bir -
swa - do ca - ca - swa - ca - ca - bird. She swal-lowed the bird to
swa - do ca - ca - swa - ca - ca - bir - swa - bir -
swa - do ca - ca - swa - ca - ca - bir - swa - bir -
71
allarg.
79
a tempo
ca - spi - Oo Ah She swal-lowed the spi-der to
allarg.
a tempo
ca - spi - Oo Ah She swal-lowed spi-der
allarg.
a tempo
ca - spi - Oo Ah She swal-lowed spi-der
allarg.
a tempo
catch the Oo Ah She swal-lowed the spi-der to
allarg.
a tempo
ca - spi-der that wrig-gled and jig-gled and tick-led in-side her. She swal-lowed spi-der
allarg.
a tempo
ca - spi - Oo Ah She swal-lowed spi-der
79
allarg.
a tempo
76

ENCORES (The Colour of Song – Vol. 4)

If You're Gonna Play in Texas
(You Gotta Have a Fiddle in the Band)

For SATTBB a cappella
Performance Time: Approx. 3:30

**Arranged by
PAUL HART**

THE EYES OF TEXAS
Words by JOHN L. SINCLAIR   Traditional Music
© 2006 The K.S. Music Co. Ltd.
International Copyright Secured   All Rights Reserved
IF YOU'RE GONNA PLAY IN TEXAS (You Gotta Have a Fiddle in the Band)
Words and Music by DAN MITCHELL and MURRY KELLUM

The eyes of Tex-as are up - on _____ you.
The eyes of Tex-as are up - on _____ you.
The eyes of Tex-as are up - on _____ you. Mm ____ Mm ____
The eyes of Tex-as are up - on _____ you. _____
Mm Mm
Mm Mm
IF YOU'RE GONNA PLAY IN TEXAS (You Gotta Have a Fiddle in the Band)
10 Country feel (♩ = ca. 84)
mf
Mm _____
Mm _____
Mm _____ Mm _____
Mm _____ I re-mem-ber down _ in Hous-ton, we were put-tin' on a show, _ when a
Mm _____ Mm _____
Mm _____
10 Country feel (♩ = ca. 84)

Mm
Mm
Mm
"Cot-ton Eyed Joe!"
cow - boy in the back stood up and yelled, He said
Mm
we love what you're do-in', boys, don't get us wrong. There's
Mm
Mm
mf
Hm
12
14

in your song.
in your song.
just some - thin' miss - in' in your song. There's
in your song.
in your song.
in your song.
16
just some - thin' miss - in' in your song. If you're
just some - thin' miss - in' in your song. If you're
just some - thin' miss - in' in your song. If you're
Dm Dm Dm
18

20
mf
Plunk Plunk (etc.)
mf
Plunk Plunk (etc.)
gon - na play __ in Tex - as, you got-ta have a fid-dle in the band. That
gon - na play __ in Tex - as, you got-ta have a fid-dle in the band. That
gon - na play __ in Tex - as, you got-ta have a fid-dle in the band. That
Dm Dm (etc.)
20
20
lead gui-tar __ is hot, but not __ for a Loui - si - an - a man. __
lead gui-tar __ is hot, but not __ for a Loui - si - an - a man. __
lead gui-tar __ is hot, but not __ for a Loui - si - an - a man. __ So,
22

Oo
Oo
Oo
Oo
If you're
Oo
Oo
Oo
Oo
If you're
Oo
Oo
Oo
Oo
If you're
Oo
Oo
Oo
Oo
If you're
ros-in up____ that bow for "Fad - ed Love" and let's all dance.____
Oo
Oo
Oo
Oo
If you're
To Coda (p. 79)
gon - na play__ in Tex - as,
gon - na play__ in Tex - as,
gon - na play__ in Tex - as,
cresc.
gon - na play__ in Tex - as,
got-ta have a fid-dle,____
cresc.
You got-ta have a fid-dle,____
cresc.
gon - na play__ in Tex - as,
Mm____
To Coda (p. 79)
cresc.

got-ta have a fid-dle,
cresc.
got-ta have a fid-dle,
got-ta have a fid-dle,
cresc.
got-ta have a fid-dle,
got-ta have a fid-dle,
got-ta have a fid-dle,
got-ta have a fid-dle,
got-ta have a fid-dle,
got-ta have a coun-try fid-dle,
28
mf
yeah,
got - ta have a hot dang coun - try
mf
yeah,
got - ta have a hot dang coun - try
mf
yeah,
got - ta have a hot dang coun - try
mf
yeah,
mf
yeah,
mf
mf
30

ENCORES (The Colour of Song – Vol. 4)

dai did-dle-id-dle ai dai
dai did-dle-id-dle-id-dle-id-dle ai
dai did-dle-id-dle ai dai
dai dai
bid-did-dle
dai - dle dai Plunk (etc.)
dai - dle dai Plunk (etc.)
dai - dle dai Plunk (etc.)
dai dai - dle ai dai did-dle dai dud-dle dai ud-dle-ud-dle ai ud-dle dud-dle
dai dai - dle ai dai did-dle dai dud-dle did-dle-ee-ud-dle-ud-dle did-dle-ee-ud-dle dud-dle
3
3

38

40

dai   da dai__ da dai dai   dai did-dle dee did-dle dee did-dle dee did-dle
dai__ da dai__ da dai dai   dai did-dle-id-dle-id-dle-id-dle-id-dle-id-dle-id-dle
dai   dai__ dai dai. So, we   dust - ed off ____ our boots,   put our
dai   dai - dle dai dai. So, we   dust - ed off ____ our boots,   put our
So, we   dust - ed off ____ our boots,   put our
So, we   dust - ed off ____ our boots,   put our
So, we   dust - ed off ____ our boots,   put our
(stamp)
45
42
44

cow - boy hats on straight. Oo
cow - boy hats on straight. Oo
cow - boy hats on straight. Bm Bm (etc.)
cow - boy hats on straight. Them Tex - ans raised the roof when Jeff
cow - boy hats on straight. Bm Bm (etc.)
cow - boy hats, Bm Bm Bm Bm Bm (etc.)
46
You say y'all all wan - na two - step, you say
You say y'all all wan - na two - step, you say
You say y'all all wan - na two - step, you say
o - pened up his case. You say y'all all wan - na two - step, you say
You say y'all all wan - na two - step, you say
48

you wan - na do - si - do.   Well,   here's your   fid - dl - in'   song   be-fore   we
you wan - na do - si - do.   Well,   here's your   fid - dl - in'   song   be-fore   we
you wan - na do - si - do.   Well,   here's your   fid - dl - in'   song   be-fore   we
you wan - na do - si - do.   Well,   here's your   fid - dl - in'   song   be-fore   we
you wan - na do - si - do.   Well,   here's your   fid - dl - in'   song   be-fore   we
do - si - do.   Well,   here's your   fid - dl - in'   song   be-fore   we
50
go.________   Here,
go.________   Here,
go.________   Here's   a coun-try fid-dle song be - fore we go.
go.________   Here's   a coun-try fid-dle song be - fore we go.________
go.________   Here,   Play it on the
go, be-fore we go.   Here,
52

f
Play it on the fid-dle.
f
Play it on the fid-dle, play it on the fid-dle.
f
Play it on the fid-dle, play it on the fid-dle.
f
Play it on the fid-dle, play it on the fid-dle.
fid-dle, play it on the fid-dle.
f
Play it on the fid-dle. Gim-me some coun - try fid-dle.
55
D.S. al Coda (p. 70)
Dai dai did-dle ai dai dai dai did - dle ai dai
Dai_ dai_ did-dle ai dai dai dai did - dle ai dai
Dm
mf
If you're
Dm
mf
If you're
Dm
mf
If you're
Dm
If you're
Dm Dm Dm
D.S. al Coda (p. 70)
mf
mf
57

CODA
cresc. poco a poco
Dai dai did-dle
Dai did - dle dai
cresc. poco a poco
Dai dai did-dle
Dai did - dle dai
cresc. poco a poco
got-ta have a fid-dle,
cresc. poco a poco
got-ta have a fid-dle,
cresc. poco a poco
got-ta have a fid-dle,
got-ta have a fid-dle,
cresc. poco a poco
got-ta have a fid-dle,
got-ta have a fid-dle,
CODA
cresc. poco a poco
59
Dai dai did-dle
hot dang coun - try
Dai dai did-dle
hot dang coun - try
got-ta have a fid-dle,
got - ta have a hot dang coun - try
got-ta have a fid-dle,
got - ta have a hot dang coun - try
got-ta have a fid-dle,
got - ta have a hot dang coun - try
got-ta have a fid-dle,
got - ta have a hot dang coun - try
61

64
fid - dle,
fid - dle,
fid - dle,
Oo
fid - dle,
Oo
fid - dle,
The eyes of Tex - as are up - on you.
fid - dle,
Oo
64
63
Dai dai did-dle ai dai did-dle ai did - dle ai dai Plunk Plunk
Dai dai did-dle ai dai did-dle ai did - dle ai dai Plunk Plunk
Dai Plunk Plunk
Dai Plunk Plunk
Dai Plunk Plunk
Dai Plunk Plunk
66

Ob-la-di, Ob-la-da

For SATTBB a cappella

Performance Time: Approx. 3:30

Arranged by
BILL IVES

Words and Music by
JOHN LENNON and PAUL McCARTNEY

* Waggle finger in mouth while singing.
ENCORES (The Colour of Song – Vol. 4)

ENCORES (The Colour of Song – Vol. 4)

- ly is the sing-er in a band.
Des - mond says to Mol-ly, "Girl, I
mf
"Girl, I
2
15
like your face," _ and Mol-ly says this as she takes him by the hand: _
Ob - la - di _
like your face," _
dm dm dm
18

21
mp
La la la la la la la la   la la la bra____ la____ la how the life goes on,___
mp
La la la la la la la la   la la la bra____ la____ la how the life goes on,___
____ Ob-la-da ____ life goes on____ bra____ la____ la how the life goes on.
mp
La la la la la la la la   la la la bra____ la____ la how the life goes on,
Chook-a (etc.)
mp
ding   ding-n ding   ding-n   (etc.)
21
mp
mp
1
2
____ goes on.   ____________ goes on,
____ goes on.   ____________ goes on,
____ Ob-la-di____ goes on,
____ goes on.____ ____________ goes on,
3
Tid-dl-a tick-a (etc.)
ding   gn ding-n ding   ding   gn ding-n ding   (etc.)
1
2

29
life goes on.
life goes on.
mp
(Marimba)
mf
life goes on.
Des-mond takes a trol-ley to the
mp
life goes on.
(Marimba)
2
Tid-dl-a tick-a (etc.)
(ding)
29
27
mf poco marcato
(Brass)
mf poco marcato
(Brass)
jewel-er's store, __ buys __ a twen-ty car-at gold-en ring. Takes __
mf poco marcato
(Brass)
2
30

* or another percussive sound

ENCORES (The Colour of Song – Vol. 4)

la how the life goes on, goes on. La la la la la,
la how the life goes on, goes on. La la la la,
la how the life goes on. Ob - la - di
la how the life goes on, goes on.
ding gn ding -n ding ding gn ding -n ding
(Marimba)
doo doo doo doo
(Marimba)
doo doo doo doo
(Marimba)
dolce
sweet home.
Tid-dl - a tick - a tick-a tick - a (etc.)
In a cou-ple of years they have built a home sweet home.
dolce
(ding) (etc.)

sim.
mf
doo doo doo doo
(Marimba)
sim.
mf
doo doo doo doo
(Marimba)
(mf)
(Marimba)
of
(4)
(mf)
With a cou-ple of kids run-ning in the yard of
45
2nd time only
f
of Des-mond and Mol - ly Jones.
f
of Des-mond and Mol - ly Jones.
f
Des-mond and Mol - ly, Des-mond and Mol - ly Jones.
f
of Des-mond and Mol - ly Jones.
f
Des-mond and Mol - ly, Des-mond and Mol - ly Jones.
(mf)
f
Des-mond and Mol - ly, Des-mond and Mol - ly Jones. Dm dm dm dm
2nd time only
f
48

ENCORES (The Colour of Song – Vol. 4)

To Coda (p. 92)
eve - ning she still sings it she's a singer with the band.
eve - ning she still sings it she's a singer with the band.
eve - ning she still sings it she's a singer with the band.
Ob - la - di
eve - ning she still sings it she's a singer with the band.
ff
(Brass)
ff
(Brass)
To Coda (p. 92)
57
59
f
(Brass)
la
f
(Brass)
la
Ob - la - da life goes on bra la
f
(Brass)
la
Chick-a chick - a (etc.)
f
dm dm dm (etc.)
59

D.S. al Coda (p. 88)
1
2
la how the life goes on. La la la la la la la, La la la la la,
la how the life goes on. La la la la la la la, La la la la,
la how the life goes on. Ob - la - di
(4)
la how the life goes on. La la la la la,
ding gn ding - n ding ding gn ding - n ding - n
1
2
D.S. al Coda (p. 88)
61
CODA
Claps
f
Brass
la
f
Brass
la
f
Brass
Ob - la - da life goes on bra la
f
Brass
la
Chick-a chick - a (etc.)
dm dm dm (etc.)
CODA

1, 2
(Cont. clap pattern)
3
la how the life goes on. La la la la la la la, la how the life goes, la
la how the life goes on. La la la la la la la, la how the life goes, la
la how the life goes on. Ob - la - di la how the life goes, la
la how the life goes on. La la la la la, la how the life goes, la
(4)
ding gn ding - n ding dm dm dm (etc.)
1, 2
3
66
(End claps)
p
(Marimba)
la how the life goes on.
p
(Marimba)
la how the life goes on.
p
(Marimba)
la how the life goes on.
p
(Marimba)
la how the life goes on.
f
p
(Marimba)
la how the life goes on.
the life goes on!
mf
Chick- a chk
p
69

The Pirate King
(from "The Pirates Of Penzance")
For SATB and Piano
Performance Time: Approx. 2:15

Arranged by
BOB CHILCOTT

Words by W. S. GILBERT
Music by SIR ARTHUR SILLIVAN

ENCORES (The Colour of Song – Vol. 4)

10
Whoa,
Whoa,
bet - ter far to live __ and die un - der the brave black flag I fly, Than
2. sal - ly forth to seek __ my prey, I help my - self in a roy - al way. I
bet - ter far to live __ and die un - der the brave black flag I fly, Than
2. sal - ly forth to seek __ my prey, I help my - self in a roy - al way. I
10
14
whoa, whoa, _ whoa, _
whoa, whoa, _ whoa, _
play a sanc - ti - mo - nious part, with a pi - rate head and a pi - rate heart.
sink a few more ships, __ it's true, than a well - bred mon - arch ought to do;
play a sanc - ti - mo - nious part, with a pi - rate head and a pi - rate heart.
sink a few more ships, __ it's true, than a well - bred mon - arch ought to do;
14
p

18
mf
whoa,
mf
whoa,
mp
A - way to the cheat - ing world go you,
But man - y a king on a first - class throne,
f
A - way to the cheat - ing world go you,
But man - y a king on a first - class throne,
18
f
p
22
whoa,
whoa,
Where pi - rates all __ are well - to - do;
If he wants to call __ his crown his own;
Where pi - rates all __ are well - to - do; But
If he wants to call __ his crown his own; Must
mf
22
f

26
cresc.
f molto rall.
whoa, —
whoa, —
live — and die a Pi - rate King,
dir - ty work than ev - er I do,
cresc.
f molto rall.
whoa, —
whoa, —
live and die a Pi - rate King,
dir - ty work than ev - er I do,
f molto rall.
live and die a Pi - rate King,
dir - ty work than ev - er I do,
cresc.
f
molto rall.
I'll be true to the song I sing, And live — and die a Pi - rate King,
man - age some - how to get through More dir - ty work than ev - er I do,
26
mf cresc.
f molto rall.
31 a tempo
f
He is! Hur - rah for the Pi - rate
mp a tempo
f
am a Pi - rate King! He is! Hur - rah for the Pi - rate
mp a tempo
f
am a Pi - rate King! He is! Hur - rah for the Pi - rate
mf
f a tempo
For — I am a Pi - rate King! —
31
8va - - - - - - - - - - -
f a tempo

35
King! And it is, it is a glo - rious thing — to be a Pi - rate
King! And it is, it is a glo - rious thing to be a Pi - rate
King! And it is, it is a glo - rious thing to be a Pi - rate
And it is, it is a glo - rious thing — to be a Pi - rate
(8va)
35
39
mp
f
King! For I am You are! Hur - rah for our Pi - rate
King! For I am a Pi - rate King! You are! Hur - rah for our Pi - rate
King! For I am a Pi - rate King! You are! Hur - rah for our Pi - rate
King! For I am a Pi - rate King!
(8va)
39

King! And it is, it is a glo - rious thing _ to be a Pi - rate
King! And it is, it is a glo - rious thing to be a Pi - rate
King! And it is, it is a glo - rious thing to be a Pi - rate
And it is, it is a glo - rious thing _ to be a Pi - rate
(8va)
43
King! It is! Hur - rah for our Pi - rate King! Hur - rah for the Pi - rate
King! It is! Hur - rah for our Pi - rate King! Hur - rah for the Pi - rate
King! It is! Hur - rah for our Pi - rate King! Hur - rah for the Pi - rate
King! Hur - rah for the Pi - rate
(8va)
47
ff

grad. dim.
(Clap)
p
54
mf
King!
Whoa,
grad. dim.
p
mf
King!
Whoa,
grad. dim.
p
King!
grad. dim.
p
King!
mf
54
2
whoa,
Pi - rate King!
59 grad. dim.
whoa,
Pi - rate King!
grad. dim.
mf
2. When I Pi - rate King!
grad. dim.
Melody f
2. When I Pi - rate King!
grad. dim.
2
59

ENCORES (The Colour of Song – Vol. 4)

Seaside Rendezvous

For SATB div. a cappella
Performance Time: Approx. 2:25

**Arranged by
PAUL HART**

**Words and Music by
FREDDIE MERCURY**

11
oo doo doo doo doo doo doo doo, be my Clem-en-tine.
melody
oo doo doo doo doo doo doo, be my Clem-en-tine.
what you feel in - side. Mean - while I ask you to be my Clem-en-tine.
doo doo doo doo doo doo dee doo doo doo doo doo doo doo doo doo
dm dm dm dm dm dm dm b-dm dm, be my Clem-en-tine.
11
17
f
doo doo doo doo doo, Oh I love you hoo hoo
melody f
doo doo doo doo doo, I love you
f
You say you would if you could but you can't. Oh I love you hoo hoo
doo doo doo doo doo,
f
dm dm dm, Oh I love you
17
f

21
mad - ly, __ hoo hoo   Brand new an - gle,
mad - ly, __ Let my i - mag - i - na-tion run a - way __   Brand new an - gle,
mad - ly, __ hoo hoo my i - mag - i - na-tion run a - way __   Brand new an - gle,
Unis.
mad - ly, __   my i - mag - i - na-tion run a - way __ with you glad - ly. Brand new an - gle,
21
25
mp   mf
high-ly com - mend-a-ble   can we do it a - gain, __ can we
mp   mf
high-ly com - mend-a-ble   sea-side ren-dez-vous.   can we do it a - gain, __ can we
Solo
mf I feel so ro - man - tic, __   mf
high-ly com - mend-a-ble   sea-side ren-dez-vous.   rum rum rum rum rum rum rum, can we
mp
sea-side ren-dez-vous.
mp   mf
high-ly com - mend-a-ble   rum rum rum rum rum rum rum, can we
25
(♮)
mp
mf

29
f
mp
do it a - gain _ some - time? Fan - tas - tic _ Oo _
f
mp
do it a - gain _ some - time? Fan - tas - tic _ Oo _
f
mf
3
do it a - gain _ Fan - tas - tic _ c'est la vie mes - dames et mes -
f
mp
do it a - gain _ ooh I like, Fan - tas - tic _ Oo _
29
3
f
mp

33
p
mp
mf
mes - dames et mes - sieurs. _ Oo _ (sniff) this time of year_
p
mp
mf
mes - dames et mes - sieurs. _ Oo _ (sniff) this time of year_
mp
mf
sieurs. Oo _ (sniff) this time of year_
Solo And at the peak of the sea - son, the Med - i - ter - ra - ne - an,
p
mf
mf
mp
mes - dames et mes - sieurs. _ Oo _ (sniff) this time of year_
33
p
mp
mf
mf

38
f On Kazoo
Oo

f On Kazoo
Oo

Solo (spoken)
it's so fash-ion-able.
f (Quasi Banjo)
Plunk plunk   plunk   plunk   (etc.)

f (Quasi Banjo)
Plunk plunk   plunk   plunk   (etc.)
dm   dm   dm   dm   (etc.)

38
f

(On Kazoo)   slow fall   (sung)
44
doo doo   doo doo

(On Kazoo)   slow fall   (sung)
doo doo   doo doo

(Quasi
Choke Cym.)   (sung)
tch   tch   doo doo   doo doo

On Kazoo   (On Kazoo)

(Quasi
Bass Drum) dm   dm   dm   dm   (etc.)

44

(On Kazoo)
(sung)
(Kazoo)
doo
doo doo
doo doo doo doo doo
(On Kazoo)
(sung)
(Kazoo)
doo
doo doo
doo doo doo doo doo
(On Kazoo)
slow gliss.
doo
doo doo
Unis. (sung)
dm dm (etc.)
50
(On Kazoo)
3
(slap knee)
(On Kazoo)
3
(slap knee)
(sung)
(Kazoo)
(On Kazoo)
Yeah yeah
yeah yeah
3
(slap knee)
(Kazoo)
(On Kazoo)
(Pop)
(On Kazoo)
50

54
58
mp
3
3
(whistle)
Solo   I feel like danc - ing
mf
mp
Rum rum (etc.)
(Raspberrry!)
mp
Rum rum (etc.)
54
58
3
3
mp
62
f
Just keep right on   danc - ing,
mp
f
mf
in the rain,   Just keep right on   danc - ing,   What a
Can I have a vol - un - teer?
f
rrr rum rum rum rum, Just keep right on   danc - ing,
Oo
Unis.
f
rrr rum rum rum rum, Just keep right on, dm dm dm dm
62
f
mp

mp
Oo
jol - ly good i - dea.
Oo
damn jol - ly good i - dea.
Oo
mp
Oo
jol - ly good i - dea.
Oo
Solo It's such a jol - li - fi - ca - tion as a
mf
Oo
jol - ly good i - dea.
Oo
66
p
so 'tres char-mant' my dear. Oo hoo oo hoo Oh, Un-der-neath the
p
so 'tres char-mant' my dear. Oo hoo oo hoo Oh, Un-der-neath the
p
so 'tres char-mant' my dear. Oo hoo oo hoo Oh,
mat-ter of fact,
p
so 'tres char-mant' my dear. Oh,
p

71
moon - light, _______ to - geth - er we'll stroll a - cross _ the sea, _
moon - light, _______ to - geth - er we'll stroll a - cross _ the sea, _
(Quasi Banjo)
(Quasi Trombone)
(Banjo)
(Trombone)
Plunk plunk plunk, Brr _____ plunk plunk plunk plunk
(Quasi Banjo)
Plunk plunk plunk plunk (etc.)
Dm dm dm dm (etc.)
71
77
rem - i - nisc - ing ev - ery - night. Mean - time _______ I ask _ you to be my Val - en - tine._
rem - i - nisc - ing ev - ery - night. Mean - time _______ I ask _ you to be my Val - en - tine._
(Banjo)
(Trombone)
rem - i - nisc - ing ev - ery - night. Plunk plunk plunk Brr _____ be my Val - en - tine._
(Drums)
(Banjo)
rem - i - nisc - ing ev - ery night. b - dm Plunk plunk (etc.)
rem-i-nisc-ing ev - ery night. Dm dm dm dm dm dm dm dm be my Val-en - tine._
77

81
You say you'd have to tell your dad-dy,
You'd have to tell your dad-dy if you
You say you'd have to tell your dad-dy,
if you
You say you'd have to tell your dad-dy,
if you
You'd have to tell your dad-dy,
(mocking)
have to tell your dad-dy,
if you
81
85
can I'll be your Val - en - ti - no,
mp
can I'll be your Val - en - ti - no, We'll ride up-on an om-ni-bus and then
3
mp
(Drums) f
can I'll be your Val - en - ti - no, We'll ride up-on an om-ni-bus and then
b-dm
3
mp Unis.
can I'll be your Val - en - ti - no, We'll ride up-on an om-ni-bus and then the ca-si - no.
85
mp
3

112
89
f
Get a new fa - cial start a sen - sa - tion - al sea - side ren - dez - vous,
f
Get a new fa - cial start a sen - sa - tion - al sea - side ren - dez - vous,
(Banjo)
Plunk plunk plunk plunk plunk plunk plunk plunk, sea - side ren - dez - vous,
(Banjo)
f
Plunk plunk plunk plunk plunk plunk plunk plunk,
Unis. mp
Dm dm dm dm dm dm dm dm dm
so a - dor - a - ble,
f
mp
93
mp
f
p
oo hoo _ sea - side ren - dez - vous.
Oo, oo
mp
f
p
oo hoo _ sea - side ren - dez - vous.
(kiss) Oo, oo
mp
f
(spoken)
3
sea - side ren - dez - vous, _ sea - side ren - dez - vous. Give us a kiss!
(Quasi Bass Drum)
Unis. f
f
sea - side ren - dez - vous, _ sea - side ren - dez - vous.
b - dm
93
f
p